THE Stars Beckoned

Edward White's Amazing Walk in Space

WRITTEN BY **Candy Wellins**

ILLUSTRATED BY **Courtney Dawson**

PHILOMEL BOOKS

PHILOMEL BOOKS

An imprint of Penguin Random House LLC, New York

First published in the United States of America by Philomel,
an imprint of Penguin Random House LLC, 2021.

Visit us online at penguinrandomhouse.com

Library of Congress Cataloging-in-Publication Data

Names: Wellins, Candy, author. | Dawson, Courtney, illustrator.
Title: The stars beckoned : Edward White's amazing walk in space / written
  by Candy Wellins ; illustrated by Courtney Dawson.
Description: New York : Philomel Books, 2021. | Includes bibliographical
  references. | Audience: Ages 4-8 | Audience: Grades 2-3 | Summary: "A
  biography of Edward White, the first American to walk in space"—
  Provided by publisher.
Identifiers: LCCN 2020047608 | ISBN 9780593118047 (hardcover) | ISBN
  9780593206249 (epub) | ISBN 9780593118054 (Kindle edition)
Subjects: LCSH: White, Edward Higgins, II, 1930-1967—Juvenile literature.
  | Astronauts—United States—Juvenile literature. | Aeronautical
  engineers—United States—Juvenile literature. | Extravehicular activity
  (Manned space flight)—Juvenile literature.
Classification: LCC TL789.85.W445 W45 2021 | DDC 629.450092 (B)—dc23
LC record available at https://lccn.loc.gov/2020047608
Manufactured in China.

ISBN 9780593118047

10 9 8 7 6 5 4 3 2 1

Edited by Talia Benamy.
Design by Monique Sterling.

Text set in Barcelona.
Artwork digitally rendered in Adobe Photoshop.

For Charlie, who shares Edward's birthday
and his passion for life —C. W.

For Tony, for believing in me —G. D.

Edward White
loved the night,
lived where stars were big and bright.

The evening sky—
so wide, so high.
Made him wonder. Made him sigh.

The twinkling stars would beckon him

till Mama called out,
"Come back in."

He'd resist,
but then he'd go,

walking back . . .
so slow . . .
so slow.

Father flew
and Edward knew,
he was born to do it too.

But in the meantime,

church and chores,

school and Scouts
and so much more.

Still the stars would beckon him

till Father hollered,
"Come back in."

He'd resist,
but then he'd go,
walking back . . .
so slow . . .
so slow.

Edward White,
bold and bright,
became a man,
prepared for flight.

Daring pilot,
brave cadet.
Three thousand
hours in a jet.

And yet those stars still beckoned him.
His friends would cry out,
"Come back in."

He'd resist,
but then he'd go,

walking back . . .
so slow . . .
so slow.

Challenges
were underway
to reach the moon, somehow, someday.

He soon joined
a group of men
who risked and dared, again, again.

Those twinkling stars
still beckoned him
till colleagues shouted,
"Come back in."

He'd resist,
but then he'd go,
walking back . . .
so slow . . .
so slow.

Edward White,
picked for flight,
stepped out from the
highest height.

Tethered 'tween
the earth and moon,
he saw those stars.
He nearly swooned.

Those twinkling stars
enraptured him
till Houston ordered,
"Come back in."

He resisted,
couldn't go.
His heart broke,
so slow . . .
so slow.

Edward White
adored this sight.
But there was more
to life than flight.

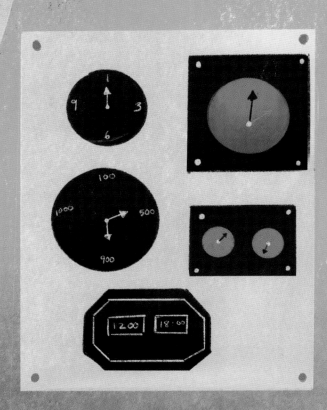

Moons and stars
are lovely places,
but not as nice as
children's faces.

For once, the earth
had beckoned him.
His children squealed,
"It's him! It's him!"

He touched down,
back home at last.
Ran to them . . .
  so fast,
    so fast.

With a blazing,

brilliant shine,

the brightest stars are most divine.

Edward White

was such a star.

He lived big and he lived far.

His country's first

to walk in space,

his steps advanced a lunar race.

From Earth below

to stars above,

Edward did it all with love.

Historical Note

ON JUNE 3, 1965, EDWARD WHITE BECAME THE FIRST AMERICAN TO WALK IN SPACE. After three orbits around the earth in the Gemini IV capsule, Edward opened the door and walked out into space. Upon stepping out, he exclaimed, "What a view! By golly . . . This is the greatest experience . . . It's just tremendous." After about twenty minutes, he was asked by the command center in Houston to reenter the spacecraft. He was enjoying himself so much that he didn't want to go back inside. Eventually, the mission's pilot, Jim McDivitt, called, "They want you to get back in now." At first, Edward laughed and replied, "I'm not coming in . . . This is fun." Finally, though, Edward reentered Gemini IV and declared, "This is the saddest moment of my life."

The Gemini IV mission was successful in many ways. The crew conducted twelve scientific and medical experiments. They proved that cabin doors could open and close in space without the spacecraft losing pressure and becoming dangerous for the astronauts inside. Edward's spacesuit and gear worked well for life outside the capsule. And the crew paved the way for future astronauts to make spacecraft repairs mid-mission. All of these triumphs led to NASA landing Apollo 11 on the moon a little more than four years later, on July 20, 1969.

Sadly, Edward was not able to celebrate the amazing achievement of the moon landing. Along with two other astronauts, he died in a fire while preparing for the launch of Apollo 1 in 1967.

Edward is remembered as a pioneer of space exploration. Since his death, he has been inducted into the International Space Hall of Fame, the U.S. Astronaut Hall of Fame, and the National Aviation Hall of Fame. On the fiftieth anniversary of the Apollo 1 tragedy, NASA opened a tribute exhibit to the three astronauts. The exhibit is titled *Ad Astra Per Aspera*, which is Latin for "a rough road leads to the stars."

Left, middle photos courtesy of NASA;
right photo courtesy of the White family

Timeline

930: Edward Higgins White II is born on November 14 in San Antonio, Texas, to Edward and Mary White. His father is an Air Force general who would serve in both World War II and the Korean War. As a boy, Edward loves sports and photography, and he is a member of the Boy Scouts.

948: Edward graduates from high school and decides to apply to the United States Military Academy at West Point. Since the school only accepts students who are recommended by members of Congress, and Edward's family has moved around so much due to his father's military career, Edward has no congressman to sponsor him. Undeterred, he walks the hallways of Capitol Hill, knocking on doors until someone gives him a recommendation.

952: Edward earns his bachelor's degree from West Point and enters the Air Force as a second lieutenant. An avid runner, Edward tries out for the US Olympic team as a hurdler. He misses the team by just one-tenth of a second.

953: Edward finishes flight school and marries Patricia Finegan. Their son, Edward White III, is born later that year. The family relocates to a US Air Force base in West Germany.

956: The Whites' daughter, Bonnie, is born. The family returns to the United States.

958: Edward earns his master's degree in aeronautical engineering from the University of Michigan. He sets his sights on becoming an astronaut and hopes the advanced degree will set him apart from other candidates.

959: Edward enrolls at the Air Force Test Pilot School at Edwards Air Force Base in California after learning that all seven astronauts chosen for the original Mercury space program were test pilots.

962: Edward is one of nine men chosen to be a member of NASA's Astronaut Group 2. Neil Armstrong is also a member of this group.

965: On June 3, Edward is the first American to walk in space. His twenty-minute space walk began over Hawaii in the Pacific Ocean and ended above the Gulf of Mexico.

966: Edward is chosen to be one of the three crewmembers of the first Apollo mission, along with commander Gus Grissom and pilot Roger Chaffee. The goal of the Apollo program was to successfully land a man on the moon.

967: On January 27, the crew of Apollo 1 is practicing a launch countdown inside the spacecraft when a fire breaks out. The cabin is filled with pure oxygen and the fire spreads quickly. The astronauts are unable to lift the latch and escape, and all three die. They are the first NASA astronauts to die while pursuing space exploration. Edward is buried at West Point Cemetery in New York.

Bibliography

"Edward White II, Astronaut Biography." NASA, https://www.jsc.nasa.gov/Bios/htmlbios/white-ed.html. Accessed 21 September 2018.

"Edward White III recalls famous father's legacy." Edward White II: The Official Website of the First American Spacewalker, https://www.cmgww.com/historic/white/blog. Accessed 21 September 2018.

Siceloff, Steven. "Apollo 1 Crew Honored in New Tribute Exhibit." NASA History. https://www.nasa.gov/feature/apollo-1-crew-honored-in-new-tribute-exhibit. Accessed 24 May 2019.

"The Glorious Walk in the Cosmos." *Life*, vol. 58, no. 25. 18 June 1965. P. 26.

"Transcript of Gemini IV mission." https://www.jsc.nasa.gov/history/mission_trans/GT04_TEC.PDF. Accessed 20 September 2018.

White, Mary C. "Detailed Biographies of Apollo 1 Crew—Ed White." NASA History. https://history.nasa.gov/Apollo204/zorn/white.htm. Accessed 21 September 2018.

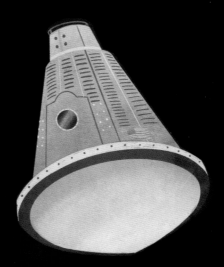